D
God's Mercy

Confession Helps for Today's Catholic

Bernard Häring, C.SS.R.

LIGUORI
PUBLICATIONS

One Liguori Drive
Liguori, Missouri 63057
(314) 464-2500

Imprimi Potest:
Edmund T. Langton, C.SS.R.
Provincial, St. Louis Province
Redemptorist Fathers

Imprimatur:
+John N. Wurm, S.T.D., Ph.D.
Vicar General, Archdiocese of St. Louis

Cover Design by Pam Hummelsheim

Acknowledgment

As with many of my previous publications, I owe heartfelt thanks to Sister Gabrielle L. Jean of the Gray Nuns and to Mrs. Josephine Ryan for their help in typing and editing this book, and for their constructive suggestions about the topics to be treated.

Bernard Häring, C.SS.R.

Table of Contents

PART THREE
Communal Celebration of Reconciliation

Foreword

Much has been said and written about the sacrament of Reconciliation in recent years. People have become acquainted with the revised forms of the sacrament as well as with nonsacramental "penance celebrations." And they have gradually come to realize two things: one, that the basic elements of the sacrament have *remained the same*; two, that this new approach makes their confessions easier and better. Even the option of confessing to the priest face-to-face (instead of behind a screen) has become more popular. Many Catholics have found this approach to be more personal and helpful.

But a new problem has arisen. Having learned the correct procedures called for by the revised rite, some Catholics are falling back into routine habits of former years. There is danger that Reconciliation — despite its renewed emphasis — could very well become a mechanical task to be performed as quickly as possible.

Individual preparation, for example, might receive only scant attention. Examination of conscience might again concentrate more on external acts (the "symptoms") than on personal attitudes (the causes of sins). True sorrow and a firm purpose of amendment might be expressed in new words but with no real change of heart. And the sense of gratitude that flows from experiencing God's mercy in confession might not receive proper attention.

In this booklet, Father Häring, a revered spiritual director, faces these problems head on. He is convinced that both priest and penitent must approach this sacrament with an ever-deepening attitude of prayer.

In *Part One,* Father Häring treats the basic attitudes or dispositions for better confessions. Each brief presentation is followed by a prayer which captures his vision. The hope is that readers will make these prayers their own.

Part Two takes the reader step-by-step through an individual confession. The emphasis is on prayerful preparation and a truly personal examination of conscience based on the Lord's Prayer. (One other form of examination, presented in Part Three, is also referred to in this second part.) The focus, after confession, is on God's limitless mercy, expressed in a prayer of gratitude.

Part Three underlines the great value of celebrating Reconciliation in community. This part of the booklet can be used by priests conducting communal celebrations of Reconciliation. Part Three is also a practical aid people can use to participate more fully in these services.

Father Häring is well known for his many theological books which accentuate the love of God. Here he shows us in a very practical and prayerful way how to share more fully in God's mercy.

> Christopher Farrell, C.SS.R.
> Editor-in-chief,
> Book Department,
> Liguori Publications

Introduction

The sacrament of Reconciliation — or Penance, as it was called in past centuries — is nothing less than a precious pearl. The person who discovers its full beauty is really blessed!

For too long this sacrament has been hidden behind clouds of misunderstanding. But today, that situation is changing. Many people are beginning to discover the truth about it. They have begun to see it for what it is: a sacrament of liberation, joy, and praise.

Reconciliation is a sacrament that can heal hurts and restore healthy relationships. It is a sacrament of continuing growth — growth in closeness to God and deepening oneness with our family.

In this sacrament we can experience what it means to be blessed — what it means to praise the Lord for suffering and dying to make us free again.

Reconciliation can lead us, in humble gratitude, to the Eucharist. It can lead us to praise God for his saving grace and for the gift of peace. It can make us instruments of peace and of all-embracing justice.

All of this may sound too good to be true. But if we enter into this sacrament with our whole heart, this Good News becomes the reality of our lives. The sacrament of Reconciliation does demand ongoing conversion, sorrow for sin, and humble confession. But this turns out to be gladdening news. For it is through sorrow that the Lord awakens in us the praise of his mercy. It is through humble confession that we come back home to the healing truth.

This booklet, then, is meant to help priests as confessors and people as penitents to become more aware of their need to heal and to be healed. By understanding and concelebrating this wonderful sacrament with renewed awareness of God's gracious love, we can enrich the world.

PART ONE

Basic Attitudes and Prayers for a Better Confession

1
Confession Praises God's Mercy

Happy is he whose fault is taken away,
  whose sin is covered.
Happy the man to whom the LORD imputes not guilt,
  in whose spirit there is no guile.
As long as I would not speak, my bones wasted away
  with my groaning all the day,
For day and night your hand was heavy upon me;
  my strength was dried up as by the heat of summer.
Then I acknowledged my sin to you,
  my guilt I covered not.
I said, "I confess my faults to the LORD,"
  and you took away the guilt of my sin.
For this shall every faithful man pray to you
  in time of stress.
Though deep waters overflow,
  they shall not reach him.
Be glad in the LORD and rejoice, you just;
  exult, all you upright of heart.

(Psalm 32:1-6,11)

People of all religions have tried to appease God by performing rituals and reciting magic formulas. But the Good News of Christ, foreshadowed in the Old Testament, is that *God* takes the initiative. He reconciles *us*. Saint Paul makes this point very clearly. Speaking of God's reconciling action, he writes: "All this has been done by God, who has reconciled us to himself through Christ and has given us the ministry of reconciliation. I mean that God, in Christ, was reconciling the world to himself, not counting men's transgressions against them, and that he has entrusted the message of reconciliation to us" (2 Cor 5:18-19).

Saint Paul was God's perfect choice for this ministry of reconciliation because of the unique way in which he was called to friendship with Christ. Paul knew what it means to experience undeserved grace.

We do not confess our sins because we think that God is a threatening God; we confess them to praise his mercy. But this praise is absolutely necessary. Our gracious God grants his gifts only to those who acknowledge them as undeserved. When we confess our sins we show our trust in God — a trust that, in itself, is praise. It is precisely this trust that enables us to face our shortcomings, our faults and sins, and to speak out sincerely.

This speaking out in open confession, or before a brother in Christ, is a liberating experience. Talking about our sins can be a frustrating, humiliating experience. But if we do it together in praise of God's mercy and healing power, then it becomes an experience of trust and liberation from anguish.

We come to the Father as brothers and sisters because we know of his compassionate love. "I will break away and return to my father, and say to him, Father, I have sinned against God and against you" (Lk 15:18). We go to our Father confessing that we are not worthy to be called his children. Yet we dare to say, "Father . . . dear Father." We say it united with Christ who entitles us to call the all-holy God our Father.

The realization that God is the Holy One and that we are sinners does not diminish the joy of our expression, "Abba, our Father." Rather, these words reveal what an undeserved gift we possess. Our Lord Jesus Christ sets us free from sin and anguish, so that we can call God "dear Father" with total trust and praise.

Through trusting prayer and humble confession we honor God. We profess our faith in him who is holy and at the same time merciful. We confess our sins because we know that his saving justice means peace, healing, liberation.

We are no better than other sinners, just as Israel was no better than other nations. The Israelites praised God for liberating Israel whenever they called upon him as their Liberator. Confessing our sins, we too praise the Father for the liberating death and Resurrection of Christ.

In the ancient Church, during the reconciliation service of Holy Thursday, the Bishop of Rome sang the Great Preface which extolled the mercy of God throughout history. In the sacrament of Reconciliation, each of us puts our own history of grace and sinfulness into the great flow of God's redeeming action. Confessor and penitent join their hearts and voices in gratitude.

Until the twelfth century the absolution was given in the form of a prayer of supplication leading to praise. The penitent who humbly confesses becomes one with the priest who also confesses his sins. Thus absolution (proclaiming God's mercy and healing power) and confession (followed by praise) are one. Priest and penitent experience a bond of oneness as sinners who accept their vocation to become saint-penitents, holy people. They are one in their praise of God.

Lord, I thank you,
for you do not want to see me ashamed
and rejected at the Last Judgment.
You want to free me from my guilt
in a very kindly way.
You do not confront me
with a ruthless or meticulous human judge
but with a brother and friend
who has the mission to help me
to know better your healing love
and to join me in the praise of your mercy.
I pray to you: Help all confessors
to be, for me and for others,
a true image of your kindness and mercy,
so that we may praise you together.
Amen.

2
Accepting Responsibility for Our Faults

**Steady your hearts, because the coming of the Lord is at hand.
Do not grumble against one another, my brothers, lest you be
condemned. See! The judge stands at the gate. As your models in
suffering hardships and in patience, brothers, take the prophets
who spoke in the name of the Lord. If anyone among you is
suffering hardship, he must pray. If a person is in good spirits, he
should sing a hymn of praise. Hence, declare your sins to one
another, and pray for one another, that you may find healing.**

The fervent petition of a holy man is powerful indeed.

(James 5:8-10,13,16)

The story of Adam and Eve (of sinful man and woman) is our
story. God gave Adam and Eve to each other as equals, as gifts
to each other. But they refused to accept themselves and one
another as gifts of God. Then, when their troubles began, they
excused themselves by blaming someone else. ''The man
replied, 'The woman whom you put here with me — she gave
me fruit from the tree, and so I ate it.' The Lord God then asked
the woman, 'Why did you do such a thing?' The woman
answered, 'The serpent tricked me into it, so I ate it' '' (Gn
3:12-13).

When he rebels against God, the man begins to despise the
woman; she is the scapegoat on whom he hangs his own faults.
The woman, in turn, blames the miserable serpent. The story
rings true to experience: people who do not confess their sins
before God and before each other always try to excuse
themselves by accusing and degrading others.

Our confession of sins is truthful and earnest if we have the
courage to accept our faults and acknowledge them before

those whom we have grieved. The sacrament of Reconciliation becomes "adoration in spirit and truth" when we confess humbly and stop accusing others. By acknowledging our faults *as our own* we restore truthful, healthy relationships.

This kind of confession differs greatly from mere ritualism, the using of confession as a kind of magic rite. There are people who confess in a dark confessional to an unknown priest *in order to avoid accepting responsibility* for the faults they are confessing. That type of ritualistic confession differs greatly from confessing in order to praise God's mercy. And if the priest is sometimes able to say, "What you have confessed is a difficulty I have too," penitents will find more courage to accept responsibility in daily life and to ask forgiveness instead of blaming their troubles on others.

The sacrament of Reconciliation is divinely instituted. But its special form arises from various beginnings and traditions. There is a clear distinction between the "Canonical Penance" imposed for gravely scandalous sins — as was the practice in the first centuries — and the confession of sins to the praise of God's mercy.

The Canonical Penance had a dimension of judgment and demanded reparation of the grave scandal. But confession to the praise of God's mercy is mainly the experience of Christ's healing power. This kind of confession probably began in the time of the apostles through the experience of fraternal correction about which the letter of Saint James speaks in chapter 5, quoted above.

A clear text on fraternal correction is Galatians 6:2. The letter to the Galatians is Paul's great message of true liberty and liberation in Christ. Fraternal correction is a sign of mutual freedom and saving solidarity.

Paul helps us to discern the harvest of the Spirit — love, joy, peace, kindness, goodness, gentleness. And he helps us to see the opposite: an ingrained egotism rooted in one's thought patterns and constantly increased by acts of selfishness. Paul's message is that, in Christ, we have that freedom which allows the Spirit to bring forth in us the harvest of goodness, justice, peace.

It is in this context that Paul proposes mutual encouragement and fraternal correction as signs of our solidarity in Christ. "Let us never be boastful, or challenging, or jealous toward one another. My brothers, if someone is detected in sin, you who live by the spirit should gently set him right, each of you trying to avoid falling into temptation himself. Help carry one another's burdens; in that way you will fulfill the law of Christ" (Gal 5:26 — 6:2).

Genuine fraternal correction is neither condescending nor disparaging. On the contrary, true healing is offered very gently and in full awareness that we, too, need it.

The eighteenth chapter of Saint Matthew's Gospel gives us deep insights about reconciliation and fraternal correction. "If your brother should commit some wrong against you, go and point out his fault, but keep it between the two of you. If he listens to you, you have won your brother over" (Mt 18:15). Jesus speaks of the readiness to forgive our brothers not only seven times but even "seventy times seven times" (Mt 18:22). This means unlimited willingness to forgive and to heal. The experience of the Lord's forgiveness and a grateful remembrance of all he has forgiven us enable us to offer gentle and effective mutual help, encouragement, and correction.

In the same context, the Lord speaks of the power of shared prayer. "Again I tell you, if two of you join your voices on earth to pray for anything whatever, it shall be granted you by my Father in heaven. Where two or three are gathered in my name, there am I in their midst" (Mt 18:19-20). This prayer is effective and pleasing to God if it comes from humble and contrite hearts joined in the confession of sins and in the praise of God's mercy.

In the thirteenth century, Saint Albert the Great and Saint Thomas Aquinas synthesized a long-standing tradition. They wrote that confession even to a lay person has a share in the sacrament of Reconciliation. However, there are certain conditions. The correction must be offered very gently and humbly. The one in need must finally accept it in humility. And the parties concerned must join in the prayer for forgiveness and in the praise of God's mercy, recognizing that forgiveness is God's gift.

This ideal is still alive in the Oriental Churches. People may go spontaneously to a holy man or woman to confess their sins and to ask for the good person's prayer. Lay people, however, were never and are not now entitled to celebrate the sacrament liturgically.

Since the first centuries in the Church, people have gone spontaneously to priests to confess sins that were not submitted to Canonical Penance. Priests were chosen from among people specially endowed by the Spirit. Remember the words of the Risen Lord, spoken in a solemn moment: "Receive the Holy Spirit. If you forgive men's sins, they are forgiven them; if you hold them bound, they are held bound" (Jn 20:22-23).

Fraternal correction and confession to the priest do not exclude each other. They complement each other. A genuine experience of fraternal encouragement gives us a better understanding of the sacrament of Reconciliation in a liturgical setting. And conversely, in celebrating the sacrament more truthfully and personally, we are helped to rediscover the value of fraternal correction.

The rediscovery of fraternal encouragement can ease the current crisis facing the sacrament of Reconciliation. The two together — each in its own way — are blessed means to bring us closer to that freedom for which Christ has set us free. They can help us to stop blaming our troubles on others and excusing ourselves by accusing others. Liberated from conceit and jealousy, we can then help each other on our road toward holiness in mutual understanding and encouragement.

Lord Jesus,
When you met sinners, you offered them trust.
When you said, "Sin no more,"
you had already told them, "Your sins are forgiven."
You corrected the faults of your apostles
but in a way that they felt your friendship even more,
and desired to become more worthy of it.
Let me receive kind and helpful correction
and encouragement through your friends,
and learn to offer it to others who need it.
Amen.

3
Examination of Conscience
Heals Hurt Memories

Remember me, O LORD, as you favor your people;
   visit me with your saving help,
That I may see the prosperity of your chosen ones,
   rejoice in the joy of your people,
   and glory with your inheritance.
We have sinned, we and our fathers;
   we have committed crimes; we have done wrong.
Our fathers in Egypt considered not your wonders;
They remembered not your abundant kindness,
   but rebelled against the Most High at the Red Sea.
Yet he saved them for his name's sake,
   to make known his power.
Save us, O LORD, our God,
   and gather us from among the nations,
That we may give thanks to your holy name
   and glory in praising you.

(Psalm 106:4-8,47)

The examination of conscience before taking part in Reconciliation can have a healing effect on our memories. But this does not happen automatically. It happens only when we examine our lives in the Lord's presence, praising his mercy toward us.

Some people tend to excuse themselves when they examine their conscience. When they recall things that hurt them, they immediately blame others for what happened. As a result, they become more angry and more bitter. Their memory of what happened becomes more distorted. When this takes place in an examination of conscience, the effect is harm, not healing.

In the sacrament of Reconciliation, the Risen Lord wants us to share his *new life* from this moment onward. When we recall our sins with this awareness, a healing of past hurts can take place. Thanking God for the good in our lives (rather than blaming others for the bad) takes away hurt and resentment that lie buried in our memories.

To recall our sins *only* as sins can cause us further harm. But when we recall them while praising God for the good in our lives, when we recall them with the purpose of praising his mercy toward us — that is a healing event. It makes examination of conscience a part of redemption. It builds healthy relationships and deepens the sense of joyful freedom Christ wants us to have.

When our memories are healed in this way, recalling our sins can make us compassionate, more understanding, more ready to forgive the sins of others. This experience of forgiveness heals us to the point where the memory of past hurts we have suffered no longer causes us harm. All the hurts and bad memories are gathered up in the renewing, redeeming power of divine mercy and forgiveness.

Lord, I thank you
for the Eucharist and all your sacraments.
In them you remind us of all your blessings upon us
and create in us a grateful memory.
When I go to confession, help me to remember,
along with my sins,
all the marvels you have done for us.
And when others offend me,
I will never remember the offense
without remembering also
that you have forgiven me all my sins
and call me to heal hurt memories.
Amen.

4
Developing a Realistic Conscience

Before faith came we were under the constraint of the law, locked in until the faith that was coming should be revealed. In other words, the law was our monitor until Christ came to bring about our justification through faith. But now that faith is here, we are no longer in the monitor's charge. Each one of you is a son of God because of your faith in Christ Jesus. All of you who have been baptized into Christ have clothed yourselves with him. There does not exist among you Jew or Greek, slave or freeman, male or female. All are one in Christ Jesus.

(Galatians 3:23-28)

In the sacrament of Reconciliation the Lord calls each of us by our own names. He summons us to meet him as friends in an intimate relationship. Whether we receive all the peace and blessing of this sacrament depends very much on how we relate to Jesus.

In the area of conscience, one of the most important contributions of humanistic psychology is the distinction between the not-yet-developed conscience and its later development as a true conscience. Psychologists point out that some persons never leave this first level; and because they do not grow or mature morally they do not develop a true conscience.

Children's personalities develop in stages. They learn to keep clean or to be quiet through the reactions of their parents or guardians. Children's egos react to approval and disapproval, to praise and blame, to reward and punishment. They are in dire need of approval. They live by approval and are shaken and threatened by disapproval.

Children's young egos seek unselfish, abiding love from their parents or guardians. They seek the security of knowing that they are loved even when there is temporary disapproval. If they do not perceive this abiding love — as is the case when parents act like moralistic policemen — the children's true egos will not develop. Parents who only *train* their children do not develop their true consciences.

Parents or guardians find order and discipline to be of great value. But if they rely too much on them, the child's true self has little chance to develop. This level of order and discipline must be allowed to develop into a relationship of trust, of being-with and being-for each other.

These psychological findings can help us to understand at least one aspect of the present crisis regarding the sacrament of Reconciliation: the case of children who are forced to confess at too early an age and under rigid conditions.

Some children have been trained to make confessions based on "grocery lists" of sins. And some priests, instead of sharing a sense of trust and acceptance by the Lord, have acted like cross-examiners when hearing the children's confessions. When these influences are at work on children whose consciences are not fully developed, the danger of stunted development is great. Later, in their adolescent and adult years, they confess on the level of an undeveloped conscience — which they do because they view confession as a duty, a meeting with a prosecutor working for a divine judge. Some finally outgrow this attitude toward Reconciliation. But if they outgrow it without gaining a deeper appreciation of the sacrament, they unconsciously or consciously abandon confession.

It is vitally important to keep little children from viewing the sacrament of Reconciliation as a method of interrogation or control. Children need to experience the priest as a friend who embodies Christ — the Divine Friend who accepts them as they are, with all their weaknesses and their need to grow.

Lawrence Kohlberg, an authority on the psychological development of conscience, is convinced that many people never outgrow the level of order and discipline, the level of "nice girl," "good boy." For these people, the sacrament of Reconciliation fulfills an early childhood need; they confess their sins in order to be "right again" before the law. The problem with this attitude is that it does not help them to overcome their sins. The moment they forget "the judge" or one of his guards, they fall back into their old ways. Then their undeveloped conscience tortures them with guilt feelings from which they find "relief" all over again by confession.

This is not at all what Christ meant by the sacrament of Reconciliation. Jesus intended it to be a personal encounter that restores a person's sense of dignity, trust, and strength. So in the sacrament of Reconciliation, the point is not to confess sins before "a court of law." The thing to do is to talk about our life with its ups and downs, and about how we cope with various situations and use our many opportunities of grace for doing good. And, looking at our failures in some of these areas, we ask forgiveness and seek the grace to become more alert and ready for future opportunities.

We do not confess our sins just to be "within the bounds of the law." We confess in order to live a relationship of trust with the gracious Lord, to grow in our desire to be healed from selfishness and to build healthy relationships with others and with ourselves.

Experiencing Reconciliation in this way, we gradually come to realize that the Lord is calling us to be partners in his work of art — his project of making each of us a wonderful masterpiece. Our role in this artistic creation is to keep discovering our own inner resources and the needs of others, to realize more profoundly that the Lord wants us as partners in the ongoing history of redemption. Once we experience Reconciliation in that way, then we can accept this vocation of ours with renewed courage and enthusiasm.

When we celebrate the sacrament of Reconciliation in this spirit, we are channeling our energies in the direction God is beckoning us. Our key concern then is not whether we are being approved or rewarded or punished, but whether we are pleasing the Lord and acting as partners in the wonderful work of redeeming, liberating, and building the family of humankind. To love and affirm others, not to win their approval, becomes our concern.

When we arrive at this point, we are no longer like "pillars of salt," looking backward. We are now moving *forward,* drawn by the God of history who gives us freedom to grow, to trust, and to share creatively in the ongoing renewal of society and human relationships.

Lord, I thank you
for the gift of faith and for your friendship.
You call me by my own name,
just as on the first Easter day
you called Mary Magdalen by her name,
and she recognized you.

You guide us by the gift of your Spirit
who prepares our hearts to promote the kingdom
of your love, peace, and justice,
and to help our neighbor.

Lord, call me!
Draw me to your heart
so that I may no longer be a slave
looking for reward
or fearing punishment from the powerful
or seeking approval of the crowd.
Amen.

5
Freeing Ourselves to Enter God's Kingdom

My brothers, remember that you have been called to live in freedom — but not a freedom that gives free rein to the flesh. Out of love, place yourselves at one another's service. The whole law has found its fulfillment in this one saying: "You shall love your neighbor as yourself." If you go on biting and tearing one another to pieces, take care! You will end up in mutual destruction!

My point is that you should live in accord with the spirit and you will not yield to the cravings of the flesh. The flesh lusts against the spirit and the spirit against the flesh; the two are directly opposed. This is why you do not do what your will intends. If you are guided by the spirit, you are not under the law. It is obvious what proceeds from the flesh: lewd conduct, impurity, licentiousness, idolatry, sorcery, hostilities, bickering, jealousy, outbursts of rage, selfish rivalries, dissensions, factions, envy, drunkenness, orgies, and the like. I warn you, as I have warned you before: those who do such things will not inherit the kingdom of God!

In contrast, the fruit of the spirit is love, joy, peace, patient endurance, kindness, generosity, faith, mildness and chastity. Against such there is no law! Those who belong to Christ Jesus have crucified their flesh with its passions and desires. Since we live by the spirit, let us follow the spirit's lead.

(Galatians 5:13-25)

The sacrament of Reconciliation is a sacrament of conversion, of turning away from the bondage of sin and turning heart and mind and conduct to God. The Bible, using the image of exodus, speaks frequently of this conversion, this setting out firmly in the direction of God's kingdom. Each time we celebrate the sacrament of Reconciliation, we should courageously enter into the great history of exodus, becoming pilgrims on the road to the kingdom of God.

Look at Abraham, at Moses and the Israelites, and at Jesus. Abraham, called by God, leaves behind an old culture — a superior culture but also an arrogant one. Setting out for the country the Lord has promised, and accepting the risk of trusting in God, he gains a new freedom. New horizons of faith open up to him.

Moses and the Israelites leave behind the bondage of Egypt. They abandon the fleshpots and the stable security granted even to slaves. They set out because Moses trusts in God's promises. He believes in liberation and liberty, in a God-given covenant that will unite the Israelites, making them free and responsible before their God.

Jesus lives the exodus anew in its very fullness. He shuns external security, wealth, comfort, and earthly glory. He resists the popular messianic expectation of a here-and-now kingdom marked by success and power, war and victories. He disavows any abuse of religion for individual or collective advancement. His whole life is an exodus, a leaving-behind. He finds the fullness of life in the word of God while living in the desert and in proclaiming the Good News to all who will listen. Then, driven out from Jerusalem by the rulers of his people, he completes the final exodus on Mount Calvary. His painful exodus brings to all people the kingdom of God — a kingdom of love, of true freedom, of friendship, trust, and peace.

The sacrament of Reconciliation is a call to creative detachment, a call to put to death all forms of selfishness, individual and collective, and thus to follow Christ in his exodus on the road of his Cross.

In his epistle to the Galatians, Paul traces the exodus from ritualistic ways of ''playing it safe,'' into the reign of true freedom. He clearly unmasks forms of conduct that must be left behind because they obstruct true freedom. The goal of this exodus is the promised land that Paul describes as the harvest of the Spirit, a new life wherein we join God in his love for his people. This new life is the kingdom of the Servant Messiah who draws us all to the Father by his gentleness, kindness, goodness.

Each of us needs an exodus from our own ingrained, accumulated selfishness. But we need also a joint exodus from all the social pressures and attitudes that tend to enslave us in today's world. We need to leave behind the many distortions of freedom in our "me first" culture that tempts us to seek "fulfillment" at the cost of friendship, fidelity, and social justice.

Only by rejecting the counterfeit freedom that feeds our selfishness can we return home to God's gift of true freedom — a freedom that builds our sense of gratitude and concern for others.

Only by rejecting shallow slogans, attitudes, and distractions can we liberate ourselves from forms of recreation that leave us no time for recollection or profound meditation. This rejection is the exodus that leads us to our true selves and opens the door to life-giving truth.

Only by rejecting the pressures of our success-oriented society — which cares more for having and using than for being and loving — can we free ourselves from a consumerism that programs us into having all kinds of artificial needs. This rejection is the exodus in which we discover our own and our neighbors' true needs.

Only by rejecting the cult of violence that bombards us on TV can we liberate ourselves from the attitude that the normal solution to conflict is greater violence. This rejection is the exodus of Christ, the Servant of God, through whom we find the promised land of gentleness, understanding, and grateful reconciliation.

We are called to reject the superficial wisdom that has us reaching for drugs as the accepted means of reducing normal frustration, the culture that opts for the abuse of alcohol and nicotine over self-possession and health. This rejection is a giant step on the exodus journey to the kingdom of true joy and freedom in the Lord.

We are called to reject the nonculture that offers cheap sex at a high price, where persons degrade, hurt, and even destroy each other. We are called to reject faddish attitudes that justify — even glorify — homosexuality, extramarital sex, and marital infidelity. We are traveling in the opposite direction: to the kingdom of goodness, fidelity, reliability, and mutual respect. Our joint search is for greater truth and surer justice — not for their opposites.

We are called to outgrow resentment, feelings of hatred and animosity. Christ beckons us to learn from his own benevolence, kindness, and true friendship.

On our exodus there is no room for sloth, inertia, or security blankets. We accept responsibility on our journey by having a true commitment among ourselves to creating peace and justice — to living faithful lives in the light of Christ, the Redeemer of the world.

In casting off all these forms of bondage and selfishness, we are not turning our backs on the world of our brothers and sisters. We are on this exodus in order to return to them as reconciled people, in order to join hands and hearts in building a homeland for justice, peace, and co-responsibility.

We have the courage to make this exodus because we have Christ as our leader and our strength. He shares with us his freedom to love, his joy, and his peace. He promises us his Spirit, the giver of all good gifts. Therefore, with trust in the Holy Spirit, we accept our call to holiness, to a life that produces the abundant harvest of the Spirit — even though this calling implies a strenuous battle against everything that opposes the kingdom of God.

If we open our eyes and hearts to the promised land of a life guided by the Holy Spirit, a life with Christ, we shall not hesitate to leave behind the alien land, the land of bondage, of selfishness, and the miserable "fleshpots" it offers us.

Lord,
I thank you for having revealed
the true nature and attractiveness
of the kingdom of God.
This is your wonderful way
of making it easier to leave behind
whatever opposes the heavenly kingdom.
Because you let me feel the beauty of your friendship,
not only have I the courage to pray
"Give me whatever leads me closer to you"
but also "Take from me whatever hinders me on the way."
Amen.

6
The Purifying Value of Sorrow

You have forgiven the guilt of your people;
   you have covered all their sins.
Show us, O LORD, your kindness,
   and grant us your salvation.
I will hear what God proclaims;
   the LORD — for he proclaims peace.
To his people, and to his faithful ones,
   and to those who put in him their hope.
Near indeed is his salvation to those who fear him,
   glory dwelling in our land.
Kindness and truth shall meet;
   justice and peace shall kiss.
Truth shall spring out of the earth,
   and justice shall look down from heaven.

(Psalm 85:3, 8-12)

At the heart of the Beatitudes is the promise, "Blest too are the sorrowing; they shall be consoled" (Mt 5:4).

In the sacrament of Reconciliation, we gratefully remember the Lord's sorrow, his Passion and death caused by our sins. It is painful to remember that we were there to cause him such great suffering. But it is consoling that the Lord suffered not in hatred and resentment but because of his enduring love and ardent compassion for us. So we praise the suffering and death of Christ, and praise the Father for having raised him up to new life.

Joining Christ in his sorrow and compassionate love for all, we open ourselves to the consolation of the Paschal Mystery. Sin causes frustrating pain. And if it is not repented, it causes distorted and destructive memories with pain that has no positive value. But by repenting we open ourselves to a new birth and a new freedom. Our sorrow, however, must be truly a participation in the sorrow of Christ. It must not be self-centered.

The sorrow blessed by the Lord is not just shame for having made a bad impression, nor is it the torture we endure as we constantly strive to save face. It is the sorrow of our true selves standing before the Lord. Our tears are genuine because we are pained by the thought that our sins have increased "the solidarity of perdition," that pressure from our society which promotes self-destructive selfishness. Our refusing to do the good that was at hand has decreased the peace and goodness on earth.

Our sorrow is blessed if it leads us to confess that the Lord's law is holy, good, just, and spiritual, and that we were unjust, ungrateful.

It is painful to realize that we are in need of conversion, a much deeper and ongoing conversion. Yet when we experience sorrow in the Lord's presence, we are consoled by the realization that conversion is possible and that the Lord will keep his promises if we accept his call to live as holy penitents.

Sorrow that unites itself to the Lord's Passion and death brings liberation and consolation. Our remorse of conscience is transformed into a purifying sorrow that gives new birth to our interest in the salvation of all people.

The overflow of that rebirth in ongoing conversion and wholesome sorrow is peace, joy, trust. And with it comes a serenity that speaks for itself and helps others to believe that they, too, are called to consolation. Then, with us, they can accept the pain of sorrow and the struggle of ongoing conversion.

Lord, send forth your Spirit
to cleanse me and to mold me.
Even if I confess my sins before you
and assure you of my contrition,

I have to be afraid of my old selfish self.
Undue concern for a good image before others
can hinder my reaching that blessed sorrow
that alone can bring me closer
to your blessed Passion and death
and to the power of your Resurrection.
Lord, grant to me and to all people
a heart truly contrite!
Amen.

7
Deepening Our Purpose of Amendment

Therefore, since we for our part are surrounded by this cloud of witnesses, let us lay aside every encumbrance of sin which clings to us and persevere in running the race which lies ahead; let us keep our eyes fixed on Jesus, who inspires and perfects our faith. For the sake of the joy which lay before him he endured the cross, heedless of its shame. He has taken his seat at the right of the throne of God. Remember how he endured the opposition of sinners; hence do not grow despondent or abandon the struggle. In your fight against sin you have not yet resisted to the point of shedding blood.

If we respected our earthly fathers who corrected us, should we not all the more submit to the Father of spirits, and live? They disciplined us as seemed right to them, to prepare us for the short span of mortal life; but God does so for our true profit, that we may share his holiness. At the time it is administered, all discipline seems a cause for grief and not for joy, but later it brings forth the fruit of peace and justice to those who are trained in its school. So strengthen your drooping hands and your weak knees. Make straight the paths you walk on, that your halting limbs may not be dislocated but healed.

(Hebrews 12:1-4, 9-13)

Traditional doctrine concerning confession has always emphasized the importance of the firm purpose of amendment. This is, as the Epistle to the Hebrews sees it, a wholehearted purpose to strive toward a holy life. And this striving for holiness is intimately connected with what theologians call "the fundamental option." Individual decisions to avoid evil or to abide by laws are not effective unless they are made as part of one's fundamental option for the Lord.

Each person born into a Christian community through Baptism is thereby introduced to God's plan outlining the fundamental option for a Christian life. And every child, being the work of the good Creator, has more innate good than evil. However, the redeemed world in which we live remains burdened by sin solidarity — the tendency in society toward selfishness and sin. As a result, we have to make a clear, fundamental option for saving solidarity in Christ.

The child who wants to love and please Christ already has this proper fundamental option. But it has to become deeper, broader, clearer, firmer. It has to take root in the person's whole character and style of life. Only in the course of growth and ongoing conversion will the fundamental option be consolidated. Each celebration of the Eucharist — and equally and particularly, the celebration of the sacrament of Reconciliation — should deepen, broaden, and clarify the fundamental option. Meaningful celebration of these sacraments reaches for that depth where the fundamental option has its center, where the Holy Spirit vivifies the spirit.

Mortal sin is a fundamental option for evil, a sin and attitude that contradicts the very depths of our commitment to Christ. If one has committed a mortal sin, it will manifest itself in the direction of decay, alienation, growing self-centeredness, arrogance, and the like. If a Christian commits a sin, but very soon or almost immediately experiences great sorrow and renews his or her fundamental option to strive toward holiness, he or she can be morally sure that the sin was not mortal. However, it might well be a serious wound, a serious sickness, a dangerous weakening of the fundamental option. If we consciously turn to Christ the Healer after each fault, in deep sorrow and in a sacramental encounter, we can hope that the distorting influence of sin is overcome and that our fundamental option has been even more strengthened.

We should make clearcut resolutions in order to fight with a positive, constructive approach against our evil tendencies.

But these concrete resolutions should be integrated into our overall resolve, the fundamental option expressed in the Epistle to the Hebrews: "Let us lay aside every encumbrance of sin which clings to us and persevere in running the race which lies ahead; let us keep our eyes fixed on Jesus, who inspires and perfects our faith" (Heb 12:1-2).

Some Christians today think that confession is necessary only if they are sure of having committed a mortal sin. This is as unwise as delaying a visit to the physician until we are sure that he can grant a death certificate. We go to the Divine Physician immediately after each sin, with an act of sorrow, a firm purpose of amendment, and great trust in God's mercy. We seek him more explicitly, more gratefully, more trustfully, and more to the praise of his mercy by a celebration of the sacrament of Reconciliation.

To gain insight into our own condition, a look at the overall direction of our life is most important. One may have committed serious faults because of ever-present passions, bad habits, the negative influence of the environment. And yet, in the overall direction, one may be ascending the scale of growth, of ongoing conversion. But we all surely need the Divine Healer to help us overcome difficulties and partial failures.

A much more serious situation would be the following. The person has not committed manifestly shocking sins, but finds himself or herself becoming more slothful, more dissipated, more self-centered because of an ever more dangerous involvement in individual or group selfishness. In such a situation there is great doubt whether the person's fundamental option is still centered on the Lord and his kingdom. The least this person should do is to turn as earnestly as possible to the Divine Healer. And normally this is done not only with acts of sorrow and humble prayer but by gratefully accepting the offer of the Divine Physician for an intimate meeting in the sacrament of healing forgiveness.

Lord, your love for us knows no bounds.
You have the right to ask of us
nothing less than a goodness without limit,
a radical resolution to seek in all things your glory
and to serve the cause of your kingdom.

By the fire of your Spirit, O Lord,
make me strong, able, and courageous in your service.
Amen.

8
Becoming One Family

I plead with you, then, as a prisoner for the Lord, to live a life worthy of the calling you have received, with perfect humility, meekness, and patience, bearing with one another lovingly. Make every effort to preserve the unity which has the Spirit as its origin and peace as its binding force. There is but one body and one Spirit, just as there is but one hope given all of you by your call. There is one Lord, one faith, one baptism; one God and Father of all, who is over all, and works through all, and is in all.

Each of us has received God's favor in the measure in which Christ bestows it. It is he who gave apostles, prophets, evangelists, pastors and teachers in roles of service for the faithful to build up the body of Christ till we become one in faith and in the knowledge of God's Son, and form that perfect man who is Christ come to full stature.

Let us, then be children no longer . . . . Rather let us profess the truth in love and grow to the full maturity of Christ the head. Through him the whole body grows, and with the proper functioning of the members joined firmly together by each supporting ligament, builds itself up in love.

(Ephesians 4:1-7,11-16)

God brings his salvation to us through his covenant. It is a covenant with the people, brought to completion in Christ who is solidarity incarnate. Christ died for us all and calls all of us to unity and solidarity "that all may be one." Conversion to God, therefore, is not possible without an ongoing conversion to the people of the covenant. We cannot find God's love without joining him in his love for all people.

The basic fundamental option is a choice between solidarity in Christ (our being with-and-for one another as one people —

which is the way God intends us to reach him) and the solidarity of perdition (the influencing of one another in the direction of lonely self-centeredness). Those who want to be saved just for themselves, unconcerned for the common good, are implicitly opting for solidarity in group self-centeredness. Therefore, if we want to strengthen our fundamental option for Christ who died for us all, we must necessarily strengthen our fundamental option for fraternal love and co-responsibility.

In examining our conscience, therefore, we need to consider the first commandment to love God with all our heart in the light of the great goal-commandment: ''Love one another as I have loved you'' (Jn 15:12). We need to ask ourselves basic questions about our personal relationships: Are they healthy? Are we appreciative? Are we respectful? Do we love only those who can reward us or, as the Lord bids, do we especially love those who cannot reward us?

It is not enough to consider only healthy person-to-person relationships, the I-thou-we relationships, important as they are. We must also consider our responsibility for the *common* good, our participation in the socioeconomic, cultural, political life. Are we faithful to the great peace mission of all Christians? Are we using all the gifts God has bestowed on us for the common good? It is not only sinful to do evil deeds; it is equally evil to bury one's own talents instead of using them for the common good. The unfaithful servant in the Gospel is not accused of having done anything evil with his talents. He is condemned, or rather he condemns himself, by deciding not to use the one talent he had been given.

Christ has come not to build his own little family, but to build up the one great family of God. He calls into this family everyone created in the image and likeness of God. Hence our confession to the praise of God's mercy must lead to an ever more fruitful and ardent commitment to the common good, to the building up of the one Body of Christ. This implies our renewed responsibility in private and public life. We must ask ourselves what we can do to promote justice, peace, and honesty in social communications, and discernment in our political preferences.

Lord, I thank you
for allowing us to call your Father "*our* Father."

I thank you for admitting me to your worldwide family
with Mary, your Mother, and all the saints.
Lord, make me grateful so that I may be
a healthy, generous, and helpful member
of your great family,
and thus atone for all my past negligence.
Amen.

9
Forgiveness Gives Birth to Freedom

If you live according to my teaching, you are truly my disciples; then you will know the truth, and the truth will set you free. I give you my assurance, everyone who lives in sin is the slave of sin. **(John 8:31-32,34)**

My little ones, I am writing this to keep you from sin. But if anyone should sin, we have, in the presence of the Father, Jesus Christ, an intercessor who is just. He is an offering for our sins, and not for our sins only, but for those of the whole world. **(1 John 2:1-2)**

There are several sacraments of forgiveness. Above all others, there is Christ himself, *the* great sacrament of healing forgiveness and saving truth. He is the One pleading our cause with the Father whenever we come to him in humble confession. In him, the Church as a whole is called to be a visible and effective sign of reconciliation and healing forgiveness. This means that each of us is called to be a kind of sacrament, communicating to others the experience of Christ's healing forgiveness.

Only after having said this do we speak of the various sacraments as manifesting and bringing home to us the Church's mission to be, in Jesus Christ, a sacrament of healing forgiveness.

Adult *Baptism* is acceptance of the call to total conversion. Those who are baptized with profound sorrow for their sins, turning totally to Christ, are freed from their sins. They do not need a particular confession, since they have not yet sinned as members of the Church. The very reception of the Baptism is a confession of the need of redemption, the need and the willingness to undertake a total conversion to Christ.

The *Eucharist,* too, is a sacrament of forgiveness. Each time we celebrate the Eucharist we praise the Lord, Jesus Christ, for the blood of the Covenant that he shed for our forgiveness. We profess our faith, acknowledging our sins and our need of further purification and healing forgiveness.

The various forms of sacramental celebrations also partake of forgiveness. From time immemorial, *night vigils* in preparation for the great feasts were seen in the light of the Eucharist. They led to fuller participation in this celebration "for the forgiveness of sins." *Lenten celebrations* also were seen in this light. They ended with a solemn communal celebration of healing forgiveness and praise of the Lord's mercy. In these settings, the whole Church prayed, through her authorized ministers, for forgiveness and for that grace of conversion that makes all our life a truthful praise and thanksgiving to God.

In our own times, we have become accustomed to *individual confession;* and, since Vatican II, we are becoming familiar with *communal celebration* of forgiveness. Since they complete each other, we should seek the sacramental experience of healing forgiveness from time to time under both forms.

Individual confession should be a special encounter with Christ and should evoke a very personal dialogue with the priest whenever we feel that we are threatened by decay or regression. We should go to individual confession in order to become more gratefully aware that the Lord calls each of us by our unique name to meet him and to be reassured by him in renewed friendship. But even then we should also be fully aware that this summons is a rallying call for all to greater unity, solidarity, and co-responsibility.

When I confess my sins to a priest, a brother in Christ, I profess my faith in a God who is love, mercy, healing forgiveness, reconciliation, and peace. In confessing to a priest, I commit myself anew to this God of love and justice. He is the saving truth.

Another part of this truth is that I am a sinner. Therefore, I confess my sins before the all-merciful and all-holy God. I confess to a brother in Christ in order to assure my sincerity, to humble myself, and to manifest my faith in saving solidarity. The freedom to confess my sins before my brothers and sisters is a God-given freedom, a freedom for fuller truth. If I refuse this truth about myself, or refuse to speak out this truth, then I may never be able to profess by my life the full truth that God is love and mercy and saving justice.

Communal celebrations of Reconciliation make us aware that each sin has a destructive social (asocial) dimension. And in unison we convert to renewed co-responsibility. The communal celebration of healing forgiveness can and should open our eyes to our sins in the social realm and to the social dimension of each sin. We thus commit ourselves as individuals and as a community to greater co-responsibility and solidarity in the peace mission of all Christians.

Communal celebration prepares each person for a more fruitful reception of the sacrament of Reconciliation in individual confession. It also makes individual confession more real and fruitful since we join our efforts of conversion and the praise of God in a shared re-commitment. But communal celebration has value even without individual confession; for many people, it can be a very profound experience of total conversion — a conversion to the Lord and to the people of the covenant.

Lord, I am grateful that you have revealed
the full truth of your merciful love.
I thank you for making me aware of my sinfulness
while calling me to a holy life.
Lord, grant me the courage to live as a holy penitent
and to accept fully the truth
that I am in need of further conversion.
Make me free for your truth and through your truth. Amen.

10
Thanking God for His Mercy

On that day, you will say:
I gave you thanks, O LORD;
 though you have been angry with me,
your anger has abated, and you have consoled me.
God indeed is my savior; I am confident and unafraid.
My strength and my courage is the LORD,
 and he has been my savior.
With joy you will draw water at the fountain of salvation,
 and say on that day:
Give thanks to the LORD, acclaim his name;
 among the nations make known his deeds.

(Isaiah 12:1-4)

In the Gospel of Saint Luke no story of healing and forgiveness ends without thanksgiving. As a physician, Luke had special insight concerning these matters. Where there is no gratitude the gift is lost. Where there is gratitude the gifts of God are received and bear a rich harvest.

In the new liturgy for the communal celebration of forgiveness, this ancient tradition of thanksgiving has been given the importance it deserves. When a person confesses individually the confessor should therefore give spontaneous expression to this praise and thanksgiving; and the penitent should respond in like manner.

It is a long-standing requirement that the confessor offers a remedy; we normally call it the "penance." But the real remedy is not so much penance in the sense of punishment and suffering. Rather, it is gratitude expressed and deepened by our renouncing everything that hinders us on our way to God, and by accepting all the sacrifices necessary for our conversion to God and to his commandment of all-embracing love and justice.

No penance will be effective if gratitude is not the principal motive and main focus. But penances should be creative. Together, confessor and penitent will find the most creative penance if they join their minds and hearts in the praise of God's kindness and compassionate love. The penances we find in this way will repair the damage that sins have caused. They will also make us more compassionate and more generously involved in the cause for peace and justice throughout the world.

On occasions of extraordinary conversions after many years of alienation, I have refrained many times from imposing or suggesting any specific penance. Instead, I have suggested that the penitent, over a certain period of time, daily renew the intention to make each day an expression of thanksgiving for God's goodness and healing forgiveness — and to determine every evening whether all his or her thoughts, words, and deeds were in conformity with this basic motive of gratitude. In several cases penitents have written to me later or told me personally that they had first thought, "This confessor is altogether too easygoing." After several weeks, however, they realized how demanding (but also how rewarding) this remedy was.

It is in this way that the sacrament of Reconciliation leads directly to its summit and source, the Eucharistic celebration. There we experience ever more deeply that the Lord is gracious to those who praise him and are willing to offer thanks always and everywhere. The penitential rite at the beginning of the Mass should revitalize the gratitude we have experienced in the celebration of the sacrament of Reconciliation; and it should prepare us to be more willing to receive this sacrament to the praise of the Lord's mercy. Thus we learn to live our whole life in abiding gratitude, through healing forgiveness,

compassion, and generous dedication to the cause of the
kingdom of God.

I thank you, Lord, for the gift of memory
that allows me to recall all the good
you have done for me and given to me.
I thank you for the Eucharist,
the memorial of your death and Resurrection
and the reassurance of your promises.
There you teach me to experience
the liberating and saving power of gratitude.
Had I been always grateful,
I would have avoided the misery of sin.
Now I thank you
that in the sacrament of healing forgiveness
you remind me kindly
that I should thank you
for your merciful forgiveness.
Amen.

11
The Peace of Forgiveness Comes from Jesus

"Peace be with you," he said again. "As the Father has sent me, so I send you."

Then he breathed on them and said: "Receive the Holy Spirit. If you forgive men's sins, they are forgiven them; if you hold them bound, they are held bound."

(John 20:21-23)

While here on earth Jesus clearly showed that, just as he has power to heal physical ills, he has power to forgive sins. "Which is easier, to say to the paralytic, 'Your sins are forgiven, or to say, 'Stand up, pick up your mat, and walk again'? That you may know that the Son of Man has authority on earth to forgive sins" (he said to the paralyzed man), "I command you: Stand up! Pick up your mat and go home" (Mk 2:9-11).

Jesus has sent his apostles to preach the Good News and to heal. Hence an essential part of their mission is to forgive — in the name of Jesus — the sins of all who repent and humbly confess their sins. But, also in the name of Jesus, the Church must declare unforgiven the sins of those who are unwilling to forgive the wrongs others have done to them.

The words of absolution constitute a prayer of the Church for forgiveness. Because of the faith and trust of the Church, this prayer pleases God. It is a prayer in the name of Jesus that praises the Father who, through the death and Resurrection of Jesus, has reconciled the world and us to himself. It asks that God, through the power of the Holy Spirit, may cleanse us from our sins and create in us a new heart and a new spirit of holiness.

Each sacrament is a privileged encounter with Jesus. At the time of absolution, through the ministry of the Church, Christ himself assures us that our sins are forgiven. This means more than mere removal of guilt; it is a new assurance of Jesus' abiding friendship.

Praying the words of absolution brings joy to the heart of the confessor. That joy he communicates to the penitent, as a jubilant proclamation of good news to the praise of the almighty and all-merciful God. And consequently he remembers gratefully that he, as much as the penitent, lives by divine forgiveness.

How can we ever thank God enough for not only forgiving us and healing us but also for giving us a visible sign and a solemn word of reassurance! In this sacrament we are assured of the power of the Holy Spirit to cleanse us from our sins, to heal our weaknesses and to make us holy.

Lord, I thank you for offering us
this sacrament of healing and liberation
and for making us so explicitly sure
of your forgiveness and abiding patience.
Lord, I want to thank you always and everywhere
for this wonderful grace.
I will show my gratitude
by granting forgiveness to all who offend me.
Help me to put this purpose into practice.
Amen.

PART TWO

Helps for Discovering God's Mercy in Individual Confession

The revised rite of Reconciliation reminds us of the importance of this sacrament of healing. It motivates us to a more fervent service of God and neighbor. At first, people were hesitant about using the new forms, especially the option of confessing face-to-face with the priest. However, once they recognized that the basic elements of the sacrament remained the same — confessing their sins, being sorry for them, and doing penance for them — they found confession easier and more profitable.

People who choose to confess face-to-face are pleased with this more personal approach. It helps them to realize that discovering and accepting God's mercy in this sacrament demand more than exterior conformity to a set procedure. The new rite of Reconciliation emphasizes interior dispositions of spiritual growth and development.

1. Preparation for Confession

The priest prepares himself by calling on the Holy Spirit to receive enlightenment and exercise charity in administering this sacrament. The penitent should also invoke the Holy Spirit to recognize his or her sins and confess them with true sorrow and firm purpose of amendment. To make an honest examination of conscience, it should be sufficient to pinpoint your failures of love for God and neighbor as indicated in the

Ten Commandments. However, your main concern should be your attitude toward your life as a Christian, as a Catholic. Are you trying to grow in the life of the Spirit through prayer, reading, and meditating on the Word of God, receiving the sacraments, giving good example, and practicing self-denial? Reconciliation heals, yes; but it also fosters these positive aspects of Godlike living.

Here are several expressive ways to invoke the Holy Spirit:

Prayer of Preparation

Dear Lord,
in my self-gratification
I did not pay attention to you;
I did not listen to your voice.
I acted as if I had forgotten that you are my friend
and that you call me
to an ever more intimate friendship with you.
Although I ignored the truth that sets me free,
you have never forgotten me.
I know that I am written into your heart
and resting in your hands.
I know that I can always come to you,
cry to you as a child cries to his mother.
I can turn to you and trust you.
Yes, Lord, I come to you and pray humbly,
"Lord, I have sinned; heal me."

Or:

Jesus,
I remember how you met sinners,
how patient you were with your disciples,
Peter and all the others,
and how you asked Peter after all his failures,
"Do you love me more than anything else?"
So you ask me now, and, Lord, I respond,

"Yes, I want to love you with all my heart,
more than anything else."
But sin is still in me,
in many corners of my being;
it blocks me on my way to you.
So I cry to you:
"Make me free; free me for you,
so that, with you, I may be free
to love your friends,
to love all those whom you love.

Or:

I remember, Lord,
how you met great sinners
and invited even them to be your friends.
You restored in them
the sense of dignity and trust.
You made them new persons.
In Galilee and Judea, and even among the heathen,
you preached that the time had come for God
to give his people a new heart,
a new way of thinking and loving.
You assure me, too, that here and now
you want to give me a new heart,
a heart renewed, a new spirit.
Even before I begin to pray,
you desire to grant me these great gifts.
You are the Lord and your gifts must be honored.
Therefore, I want to honor your gifts
in humble supplication
and in gratitude for the gift of prayer,
for the desire that you have awakened in me.
Strengthen my faith and my trust in you.
Strengthen in me the desire to love you above all
and to love all people ever better.

Renew my heart, my imagination,
my will, my whole being,
so that I may desire and love nothing
that you do not wish for me and will for me.
Or:
Let your Holy Spirit come upon me
to open my eyes and my heart
so that I may know myself in the light of your love,
and may be able to recognize my ingratitude
and learn to be grateful.
With the blindman of Jericho,
I cry and will continue to cry:
"Jesus, Son of David, have mercy on me.
Jesus, Son of the living God, have mercy on me!
I want to recover my sight."
Not only the world around me but my own sins
have made me partially blind.
I detest my self-deceit and all my tendencies
to untruthfulness, to antagonism, to laxity.
I detest
my deception of others and my contribution
to the widespread deceit so common today.
Lord, you are powerful.
Touch my eyes, touch my heart,
and I will stop deceiving myself.
I will stop deceiving others
and allowing them to deceive me.
Or:
Send forth the Spirit of Truth
to introduce me to all truth.
Let your Holy Spirit come upon me and cleanse me,
so that I may fully accept
the saddening truth about my sins
but also recognize more fully
the consoling truth of your liberating love.

Examination of Conscience

The following examination of conscience is based on the Lord's Prayer. Another examination may be found on pages 72 through 75.

"Our Father who art in heaven"

Father, what an unheard-of privilege that, with your only begotten Son, I can call you "Father, dear Father"! What a wonderful gift that, together with your beloved Son, I can join all people in calling you "Our Father." Forgive me, Father, for I have not always proclaimed your name with all the love and trust due to you. Forgive my distrust, my doubts, my distractions when I should have been living constantly in your presence.

Your beloved Son has taught us all to adore you, the Father of all, in spirit and truth. But when I say "Our Father," I realize that I have not always loved your children in union with you and your Son Jesus Christ. I have been too concerned with myself. Yet, because the Spirit prays in each person, I could cry out "Abba, our Father." So I could also have joined you more completely in your love for all your children, in your great zeal to make humankind one family to the honor of your name.

When praying to you and remembering your name, I have all too often failed to realize fully that "you are in heaven" — you, the Holy One, and I your creature; you, the Holy One, and I, a sinner. I should remember this and be all the more grateful for your invitation to call you "Father" and to unite with all the people on earth to honor you as the Father of all.

Father, forgive me my lack of humility. Each time I pray to you in heaven, I should have deep sorrow for my sins; I should feel humble. Compared with your holiness, I should never feel exalted over others. You alone know who has received the greater gifts from your hands. You know who is the greater sinner — the one who outwardly seems to be a greater sinner or

I who have received so many signs of your love and yet have not given you all my heart and all my life.

"Hallowed be thy name"

All my being should sing with Mary, "Holy is his name; his mercy is from age to age." All my being should glorify your name, as you do by your saving justice, by your concern for people, by your compassion and mercy. It is my wonderful vocation to make known your name to others, especially to those entrusted to me. But so frequently I have been more concerned for my own honor, my own importance, than for my mission to make known your name and the name of Jesus whom you have sent to show us the full extent of your goodness, love, and mercy. I have not even given enough attention to know your name, that of "Father," and to know the name of Jesus, the Savior, the Divine Healer, the One who was, is, and will come. How, then, can I truthfully pray that your name be honored, praised, and known by all people?

Father, forgive me for having dishonored your name by placing myself first or by living a distracted life that hinders me from knowing you and finding out the unique, wonderful name by which you call me! Forgive me, Father, for not honoring and accepting some of my fellow human beings in their uniqueness, for not trying to know the wonderful, unique name by which you call them and all of us together.

"Thy kingdom come"

Father, I have prayed frequently for the coming of your kingdom, but I have sometimes been more interested in my own little world. I confess that I have not taken enough time to listen to what your Son said about your kingdom and how he showed it by his life. My prayer, "Thy kingdom come," was not sincere enough. I could not pray to have my share in it when I neglected my basic duty to know what your kingdom is like.

Yes, I do know some very important aspects of it, but I have not acted accordingly. I know that your kingdom is like the mustard seed: it grows as a result of concentrated effort and openness on the part of God's people. But so many times I have been unwilling to learn and to be more thoroughly converted. Often I have not had the patience needed for either myself or others; I have not allowed others to grow according to the measure of grace you had bestowed on them. I have frequently requested that they take the third step before the second, while not taking the step I myself should have taken.

I know that your kingdom is the reign of your gracious gift, under the law of grace. Since I have not given thanks sufficiently nor discovered all your gifts, I have been neither able nor willing to meet the real needs of my neighbors. I know that your kingdom is a kingdom of justice and peace, yet inertia or selfishness has hindered me from becoming involved in the cause of peace, unity, solidarity, and justice.

I know that your reign means gentleness, kindness, benevolence. And yet I have dared to lack gentleness with others immediately after I had prayed, ''Thy kingdom come.'' Lord, forgive me! Lord, have mercy!

''Thy will be done on earth as it is in heaven''

Father, you sent us Jesus, your beloved Son who by his words, life, and death made known to us on earth how your will is done in heaven. Yet, I have not taken enough time to look at Jesus. By knowing him better I can learn to know your loving will. Forgive me, Father! Your name is Love, and Jesus has shown us the full extent of this love. Still, I have not fervently and unceasingly implored the gift of your Spirit in order to discern true love and to keep the world from deceiving me with counterfeit love.

In Jesus Christ you called me to become your true image and likeness, a kind of sacrament to help other people to become more familiar with the true face of redeemed and redeeming love. But I have diminished your glory on earth. By my negligence many people do not know well enough how your will is done in heaven and how it could be done on earth. Father, forgive me!

Even when praying, "Thy will be done," I was stubborn. I have wanted people to do my will instead of engaging in a common search for truthful solutions to the problems of life so that your will might be done. Father, forgive me!

I have not given enough attention to the lives of the saints. I have not listened enough to the prophets who have helped to interpret your will. I have not honored enough the simple and humble ones who frequently have the best insight about how your will should be done on earth. Considering myself wise, I have refused to join the humble and simple ones to whom you reveal the secrets of your will. Father, forgive!

"Give us this day our daily bread"

Father, your beloved Son taught us to call you joyfully and intimately, "Abba, dear Father." He informed us that you are the Holy One and that we must be concerned for the glory of your name, your kingdom, and your holy will. But frequently, before rejoicing in your name while communicating with you, I have prayed for "our daily bread," meaning *my* bread. I have forgotten to pray equally for the bread, health, dignity, and justice due to all people. I have forgotten that you gave me talents to share with others so that we *all* can rejoice at the common table.

Praying for our bread, I have not been grateful enough to recognize that you have prepared the table of your Word, the table of the body and blood of Christ where we all become blood brothers and sisters. And so I have not been willing to share everything in my life, as far as I can, just as Jesus shared his life and his blood with us.

Father, forgive me for overindulging in material things for my own pleasure, unconcerned that all these things are gifts from you, the Father of all! I did not use my talents to convince my fellow citizens and neighbors to adopt a more simple life-style and not to exhaust the resources of this earth to the detriment of the poor nations and future generations. I must confess that I have not always prayed, "Give *us* this day *our* daily bread," as Jesus intended.

"And forgive us our trespasses
as we forgive those who trespass against us"

I would never dare to say to you, Father, "Forgive *me my* trespasses (sins) just as I forgive those who trespass (sin) against me." For my forgiving is imperfect. I sometimes face a hard, long struggle to free myself from resentment. But if I pray, "Forgive *us*," I know that I pray with Jesus who did forgive on the Cross. I pray with the saints, asking that you confirm me with your healing forgiveness, with the forgiveness of Jesus. And praying for your forgiveness, I sincerely express my longing to be forgiving like Jesus, to be as forgiving as you, our healing and forgiving Father. Accept this prayer of mine, and grant that my longing will grow and unfold to receive this great grace.

In the midst of the bitterness that comes from social classes and groups accusing each other and excusing themselves, I find myself at times agreeing with these attitudes. Yet I know that you have sent me to be a peacemaker, a reconciler. Father, forgive!

"And lead us not into temptation"

Father, we sinners have built up a world that has institutionalized temptations. We allow a polluted environment that brings with it temptation and degradation. While we pray that you lead us not into temptation, we know that you are not tempting us. But sometimes we forget that our prayer can be sincere only if we join actively with other people of good will to create a more humane world. Only in this way will we eliminate the temptations that come from our personal and collective selfishness, suspicion, arrogance, and pride. Father, forgive us for turning the paradise you created on earth into a chaos of great temptation for many people.

Father, if I had always responded to your grace, I would be stronger. It is my fault that I am still weak. Yet, I come to you with trust. I pray that my strength and your special grace will help me to stand firm and to grow through any test you allow to come my way. In prayer and in action, I must prepare myself through greater fidelity in everyday decisions to stand the test in the important decisions of my life.

But how can I pray to withstand temptation if I do not help others, pray for them, encourage them, and unite with all people of goodwill to remove the most dangerous temptations from our earth? Father, forgive me!

"But deliver us from evil"

The evil one, the disturber, carries on his malicious plans through unhealthy authority structures, lust for power, greed, sexism, racism. He uses each of us when we yield to these evils, whenever we are arrogant, whenever we manipulate others or allow others to manipulate us. I know, Father, that I cannot pray sincerely without repenting for all my participations in the sins of others, and for my sloth and inertia. Because my prayer was not earnest enough, I have not accepted my share of responsibility. Yet, I come to you, Father, with trust and I pray, "Father, heal me, for I have sinned!"

"For the kingdom, the power and the glory are yours, now and for ever."

Father, so often I have cried to you in my needs. Then, when you helped me, I failed to give you the glory. When my prayer did not lead into praise and thanksgiving I should have known it was faulty. The evil one and the evil world have no power over me when I turn my attention in praise, to your kingdom and power, and seek your glory above all things.

Forgive me for all the times I have given more attention to evil than to your marvelous deeds and the example of holy people. Father, forgive!

Having examined your conscience, ask now for the gift of sorrow. Then, silently and sincerely pray one of the acts of contrition that follow this prayer for sorrow.

Prayer for the Blessed Gift of Sorrow

Father,
my sins have caused great pain
for me and for others.
And this pain was not blessed;
it was self-punishment and injustice to others
for whom I should be a source of peace.

Father,
grant me the gift of blessed sorrow.
May your Holy Spirit help me
to enter into the blessed sorrow of Christ
that is a redeeming manifestation
of your compassion.

Grant me, Father,
a heart renewed with sorrow
for the damage my sins have wrought
to your kingdom,
to the salvation of the world.
Grant me sorrow
that brings forth a rebirth,
a new zeal, more compassion,
a great readiness to forgive and to heal.

Give me courage, Father,
to face my sins, even if they shame me.
Give me sorrow that makes me humble
in confession before the priest
and in my daily life.

Father,
give me that blessed sorrow
that is filled with trust in you!
Amen.

Acts of Contrition

Father, I have sinned against you
and am not worthy to be called your son.
Be merciful to me, a sinner.

Or:

Father of mercy,
like the prodigal son
I return to you and say:
"I have sinned against you
and am no longer worthy
to be called your son."
Christ Jesus, Savior of the world,
I pray with the repentant thief
to whom you promised Paradise:
"Lord, remember me in your kingdom."
Holy Spirit, fountain of love,
I call on you with trust:
"Purify my heart,
and help me to walk as a child of light."

Or:

Lord Jesus,
you chose to be called the friend of sinners.
By your saving death and Resurrection,
free me from my sins.
May your peace take root in my heart
and bring forth a harvest
of love, holiness, and truth.

Or:

Lord Jesus Christ,
you are the Lamb of God;
you take away the sins of the world.
Through the grace of the Holy Spirit,
restore me to friendship with your Father.
Cleanse me from every stain of sin
in the blood you shed for me,
and raise me to new life
for the glory of your name.

Or:

Lord Jesus, Son of God,
have mercy on me, a sinner.

2. Confession of Sins

If the direction of your life is clear and serene, your confession need not take long. You need only mention two or three matters in which you feel you should be making greater progress. Impatience, untruthfulness, a lack of charity — these are faults that plague us all.

However, on certain occasions you may have to make important life decisions. Or you may not see clearly how to cope with specific problems. At such times, it is advisable to speak with your confessor privately (or confess in the reconciliation room — where one is available). There, you will have enough time to explain your situation to the priest, in the sight of the Divine Physician, and thus find proper encouragement and advice. Beforehand, it would not be inappropriate to pray for the priest — that he will possess the attitude of the Divine Physician and join you in praising God by your humble confession and subsequent attitude toward life.

When you enter the confessional or reconciliation room, the priest will welcome you warmly. He is your friend, your brother. As a fellow human being, he knows what it means to be "wounded" by sin. After making the sign of the cross, listen and respond to him as he urges you to have confidence in God. The priest may then read or say from memory a passage from Scripture. Or you may choose a short Scripture reading on which you meditated before confession and ask to read it at this time. In this way, you can focus on a word of the Bible that has struck your heart, calling you to conversion and to confidence in God's mercy. (This reading is optional.)

When you begin your confession, indicate your state in life. For example: "Father, I'm single (married/divorced/a widow/a widower)."

Then say: "My last confession was (so many days, weeks, months, years ago)."

Next, if customary, you may say: "I confess to almighty God. . . ." Otherwise, all that is needed are these or similar words: "These are my sins." Serious sins — major wrongs committed with full awareness and total freedom — must be confessed. Tell what kind of sin it was and approximately how many times it was committed. Lesser sins need not be confessed; but to mention at least some of them helps you to conquer them and insure your growth as a Christian.

If necessary, the priest will help you make your confession. He will give suitable counsel and instruction, urging you to true sorrow for sin and amendment of life. If you have been the source of harm or scandal to others, you must resolve to make reparation.

The priest then imposes a penance. (You may suggest to the priest the penance that you feel would be most appropriate.) This will correspond to the seriousness and nature of the sins confessed. It may consist of prayer, self-denial, or works of service to others.

You now express sorrow for sin and resolve to begin a new life. This may be done in various ways. You may prefer the words of the traditional act of contrition. Or you may use your own words to formulate an act of sorrow. You could also use the following words or others like them:

My God,
I am sorry for my sins with all my heart.
In choosing to do wrong
and failing to do good,
I have sinned against you
whom I should love above all things.
I firmly intend, with your help,
to do penance,
to sin no more,
and to avoid whatever leads me to sin.
Our Savior Jesus Christ
suffered and died for us.
In his name, my God, have mercy.

3. Absolution by the Priest

After your prayer of contrition the priest extends his hands, or at least extends his right hand, over your head and pronounces the absolution. Listen prayerfully to the words.

God, the Father of mercies,
through the death and resurrection of his Son
has reconciled the world to himself
and sent the Holy Spirit among us
for the forgiveness of sins;
through the ministry of the Church
may God give you pardon and peace,
and I absolve you from your sins
in the name of the Father, and of the Son, +
and of the Holy Spirit.

After the absolution, join with the priest in explicit praise of God.

Priest: Give thanks to the Lord, for he is good.
Response: His mercy endures forever.

Finally, the priest bids you farewell in these or similar words:

The Lord has freed you from your sins. Go in peace.

4. Thanksgiving and Penance after Confession

On leaving the confessional, say your penance immediately if it consists of prayer. If it is an act of self-denial or a work of service, plan how to do it as soon as possible. Then offer a prayer of thanksgiving. Choose either of the following or fashion one of your own.

Father,
I thank you for the gift of peace,
and I want to thank you always.
Let me become a source of peace
for my brothers and sisters,
for all who need healing,
forgiveness,
patience,
kind understanding,
and encouragement.
Your peace is your gift to me,
a gift to be shared with others,
because it is prepared by your Son,
the Savior of all.
Let me experience ever more
the power of your Spirit,
so that your peace
will always abound in my heart,
marking my life
and all my relationships.

Or:

Lord God, our Father,
there is so much hatred and resentment
in the lives of so many people!
Send them peacemakers.
Help them to seek and to find you,
the source of all peace and reconciliation.
Lord, unite all of us who have experienced
your healing forgiveness and your peace,
so that together we may promote
peace and justice in the world,
in our families, our neighborhoods,
in our economic and political relationships.
Lord, let me look back gratefully on my past,
so that I may no longer be
a prisoner of my selfishness
and small worries,
but do the work of peace day by day.

PART THREE

Communal Celebration
of Reconciliation

PRENOTE. Part Three of this booklet can serve a number of purposes:

- People can use it, privately or in a group, to prepare for a communal celebration.
- Priests can use it as a text for the celebration itself.
- Families and communities can use it as a review to deepen their lives together.

However it is used, this section can foster understanding of the basic dimensions and purpose of communal celebrations of reconciliation.

When a number of penitents assemble for sacramental Reconciliation, it is fitting that they prepare for the sacrament by celebrating the word of God.

Those who will receive the sacrament at another time may also take part in the service.

Communal celebration shows the ecclesial nature of Reconciliation. The faithful listen to the word of God, which proclaims his mercy and invites them to conversion. They examine their lives in the light of God's word and help each other through shared prayer. After each person has confessed his or her sins and received absolution, all praise God's wonderful deeds on behalf of the people he has gained through the blood of his Son.

If necessary, several priests will be available in suitable places to hear individual confessions and to reconcile the penitents.

1. Entrance Song

Here an appropriate song may be sung. A psalm – for example, Psalm 100 – may be recited. Or a suitable antiphon, like any of the following, may be prayed.

Yes, I shall arise and return to my Father.
To you, O Lord, I lift up my soul. In you, O my God,
I place all my trust.
Look down on me; have mercy, O Lord, forgive me my sins!
Behold all my grief!
My heart and soul shall yearn for your face;
be gracious to me and answer my plea!
Do not withhold your goodness from me;
O Lord, may your love be deep in my soul.

2. Greeting and Mutual Blessing

A greeting similar to the following, or one from the penitential rite of the Mass, may be used.

Priest: Peace and grace from God, our Father, and from our Lord Jesus Christ, be with you all!
Response: And with your spirit!

3. Opening Prayer

As at Mass, the invitation to pray is followed by a period of silence. Then, the following, or a similar prayer, seeking conversion and the grace of repentance, may be used.

Lord,
we have come to celebrate your mercy,
to receive the good news

that further conversion is possible.
We come to manifest our faith
that we can live the Gospel
and deepen our resolution.
We want to live the Gospel.
O Lord, strengthen our faith,
that we may truly believe
with heart, mind, and life-style
that you can and want to renew our hearts
and the face of the earth.
Send us your Spirit so that we may live
in a new spirit of gratitude.
We want to believe fully in your promises
of the new heaven and the new earth
Send forth your Spirit to cleanse our hearts,
to free us from all deceit, and to help us follow
your call to holiness of life.
We ask this through Christ, our Lord.
Amen.

4. Celebration of the Word of God

When there are three readings from Scripture, the format follows that of the Sunday readings at Mass, with a responsorial psalm and an Alleluia verse. (At penitential celebrations which do not include absolution by the priest, selections from the Fathers of the early Church and other spiritual writers may be read before or after the readings from Scripture.) These readings will emphasize the following points: (a) the voice of God calling us back to conversion and ever closer conformity with Christ; (b) the mystery of our reconciliation through the death and Resurrection of Christ and through the gift of the Holy Spirit; and (c) the judgment of God about good and evil in our lives as a help in our examination of conscience. If there is only one reading, however, a Gospel selection is preferred.

Reading I   Dt 6:4-7

A reading from the book of Deuteronomy

Hear, O Israel! The LORD is our God, the LORD alone! Therefore, you shall love the LORD, your God, with all your heart, and with all your soul, and with all your strength. Take to heart these words which I enjoin on you today. Drill them into your children. Speak of them at home and abroad, whether you are busy or at rest.

This is the Word of the Lord.

R. **Thanks be to God.**

Responsorial Psalm   Psalm 31:2-6

R. **Save me, O Lord, in your steadfast love.**

In you, O LORD, I take refuge;
    let me never be put to shame.
In your justice rescue me,
    incline your ear to me,
    make haste to deliver me!

R. **Save me, O Lord, in your steadfast love.**

Be my rock of refuge,
    a stronghold to give me safety.
You are my rock and my fortress;
    for your name's sake you will lead
        and guide me.

R. **Save me, O Lord, in your steadfast love.**

You will free me from the snare they
        set for me,
    for you are my refuge.
Into your hands I commend my
        spirit;
    you will redeem me, O LORD,
        O faithful God.

R. **Save me, O Lord, in your steadfast love.**

Reading II   2 Cor 5:14-21

A reading from the second letter of Paul to the Corinthians

The love of Christ impels us who have reached the conviction that since one died for all, all died. He died for all so that those who live might live no longer for themselves, but for him who for their sakes died and was raised up.

Because of this we no longer look on anyone in terms of mere human judgment. If at one time we so regarded Christ, we no longer know him by this standard. This means that if anyone is in Christ, he is a new creation. The old order has passed away; now all is new! All this has been done by God, who has reconciled us to himself through Christ and has given us the ministry of reconciliation. I mean that God, in Christ, was reconciling the world to himself, not counting men's transgressions against them, and that he has entrusted the message of reconciliation to us. This makes us ambassadors for Christ, God as it were appealing through us. We implore you, in Christ's name: be reconciled to God. For our sakes God made him who did not know sin, to be sin, so that in him we might become the very holiness of God.

This is the Word of the Lord.

R. **Thanks be to God.**

Alleluia   Jn 8:12
R. **Alleluia.**
I am the light of the world.
    The man who follows me will have the light of life.
R. **Alleluia.**

Gospel   Mt 5:1-12
V. The Lord be with you.
R. **And also with you.**
    A reading from the holy gospel according to Matthew
R. **Glory to you, Lord.**

When he saw the crowds he went up on the mountainside. After he had sat down his disciples gathered around him, and he began to teach them:

"How blest are the poor in spirit: the reign of God is theirs.
Blest too are the sorrowing; they shall be consoled.
[Blest are the lowly; they shall inherit the land.]
Blest are they who hunger and thirst for holiness;
    they shall have their fill.
Blest are they who show mercy; mercy shall be theirs.
Blest are the single-hearted for they shall see God.
Blest too the peacemakers; they shall be called sons of God.
Blest are those persecuted for holiness' sake;
    the reign of God is theirs.
Blest are you when they insult you and persecute you and
    utter every kind of slander against you because of me.
Be glad and rejoice, for your reward is great in heaven;
    they persecuted the prophets before you in the very same way."

This is the gospel of the Lord.

R. **Praise to you, Lord Jesus Christ.**

5. Homily

The homily reflects on the readings. It leads the penitents to examine their consciences and renew their lives. It recalls the infinite mercy of God, the need for interior repentance, the social aspect of grace and sin, and the duty to make satisfaction for sin through penance and true charity toward God and neighbor. After the homily the penitents examine their consciences in silence. They remind themselves that sin works against God, against community, and against themselves. To arrive at this conviction and to awaken sorrow in their hearts the following prayer may be said alone or shared with others.

6. Personal Reflection and/or Shared Prayer

We thank you, Father, for the gift of faith.
Many generations have tried to appease you
by empty rituals.
But you have revealed to us that Christ himself
is the Reconciliation and the Reconciler.
You have taken the initiative
and it is all your work.
In celebrating the sacrament of
reconciliation together,
we want to honor your initiative
and give to you alone the glory
for restoring our peace.
All too often
we have stolen this glory from you,
thinking it was our achievement.
Yet only if we are grateful
can we share in your work,
in the healing of our wounds
and the wounds of others.
Help us to accept our peace mission in this world.

Father,
even while knowing that Christ died for us,
we have continued, time and again,
to live selfishly for ourselves,
or have made ourselves prisoners of group selfishness,
collective manipulation and deceit.
Forgive us, Father!

Father,
heal your wounded people.
Make us healers for others.

Allow us, Lord,
to become reconciled reconcilers
and peacemakers wherever we may be.
Amen.

7. Examination of Conscience

A communal examination of conscience may take the place of the homily. It should be clearly based on the text of the Scripture that has just been read. The following examination is based on the Beatitudes as found in Matthew 5:1-10.

"After he had sat down his disciples gathered around him, and he began to teach them . . ."

Lord, our life is wonderful. It is a whole new life. Our gathering together in your name, listening to your word, and living that word together for the glory of the Father — all this is a sign of the new heaven and new earth. Forgive us, Lord, for having come together so often with hostile or indifferent attitudes! Forgive us for all the times we have come together driven by personal or group selfishness! Heal us, O Lord, from the sentiments that so often keep us from really coming together, from truly being gathered in your presence.

"How blest are the poor in spirit: the reign of God is theirs."

Lord Jesus, I see you as the humble servant of God, who has made himself poor in order to enrich us. I know what your words mean, but I would know them so much better if I became humble like you and put your words into practice. Lord, forgive me my lack of humility, my lack of gratitude.

Jesus, you come from the Father and return to him with all your brothers and sisters, having shared yourself and your very lifeblood with them. Seeing you in this light, I know what it means to belong to the poor who are blessed. I would know and experience the blessedness of your kingdom more deeply if I shared, for the good of all, the gifts I have received. Teach me to share not only words but all that I have, all I can do, and my very self with my brothers and sisters. Lord, forgive me my self-centeredness and my preoccupation with group selfishness.

(Here may follow personal reflection or sharing of humble confession.)

"Blest too are the sorrowing; they shall be consoled."
Looking at you, Lord Jesus, I recognize the sorrowful who will find consolation. You and all your followers who are free from self-pity because they share in the sorrows and sufferings of all — these are the sorrowful. They are willing to bear the burden of all. They put to death their selfishness, whatever pain it may cost, and are willing to fulfill the great law of love of neighbor, accepting all the difficulties and pain involved.

(Here may follow personal reflection or sharing of humble confession.)

"Blest are the lowly; they shall inherit the land."
Looking at you, Lord Jesus, the teacher and model of true humility and gentleness of spirit, I know what your words mean. I praise you for wanting to draw people to yourself only by your gentle love and not force, threats, and power. Forgive me, Lord, my vindictive spirit, my attempts at lording it over others, my endeavors to use religion for my own advantage or that of my group. Lord, forgive!

Israel would have been saved had your people accepted your gentle rule, the rule of your kingdom. Jerusalem would not have been destroyed had its people learned from you the gentle but irresistible power of nonviolent love. The terrible sufferings of world wars would have been spared had Christians followed you in your nonviolent love, your gentle reign, in a common commitment to justice and peace. Lord, forgive!

(Here may follow personal reflection or sharing of humble confession.)

**"Blest are they who hunger and thirst for holiness;
they shall have their fill."**

Looking at you, Lord Jesus, again I know what your words mean. But I would know you better if I were more grateful for your saving grace. And I would find more fulfillment in my life if I followed you in your concern for all people, for the holiness which creates social justice on all levels everywhere. Lord, forgive!

(Here may follow personal reflection or sharing of humble confession.)

"Blest are they who show mercy; mercy shall be theirs."

Looking at you, Lord Jesus, I truly know the meaning of your command, "Be compassionate, as your Father is compassionate." If I am merciless in spite of your saving justice, in spite of your compassionate love manifested on the Cross even to your enemies — then I deserve a merciless judgment; indeed, I punish myself. It is a duty of justice, Lord, to follow you in your merciful love. Lord, forgive me for being, so often, hard of heart!

(Here may follow personal reflection or sharing of humble confession.)

"Blest are the single-hearted for they shall see God."

Looking at you, Lord Jesus, I see the Father. And if I turn my eyes, mind, heart, and will only to you and serve you with unselfish intentions, I will know you and your Father better and find total salvation in this saving knowledge. Lord, forgive my selfishness. Forgive me for using and even misusing others under the guise of love!

(Here may follow personal reflection or sharing of humble confession.)

"Blest too the peacemakers;
they shall be called sons of God."
Lord Jesus Christ, you have brought reconciliation and peace at the cost of your precious blood. Seeing you in this light, I know what it means to be a peacemaker. I see how you honored the Father so trustfully — even on the Cross — by entrusting your Spirit to him. You honored the Father by praying for those who had scourged you, wounded you, crucified you. You prayed for those who, by their sins, would become your enemies; and because of this I know how a child of God should act. Lord, forgive me for so often failing to fulfill my great peace mission on earth and thus making myself unworthy to be called a child of our heavenly Father!

(Here may follow personal reflection or sharing of humble confession.)

"Blest are those persecuted for holiness' sake;
the reign of God is theirs."
Looking at you, Lord Jesus, I know what it means to share in the kingdom of God by suffering for the sake of holiness. If I were grateful enough, I would understand that persecution deepens my fidelity to the divine precepts through which holiness is attained. Then, I would be ready, as you were, to suffer whatever might come in my mission to make the Father's holiness a visible reality. Lord, forgive my unwillingness to suffer for the cause of right! Forgive my reluctance to give up the privileges I share with people in my circle so as to prove my faith in the one God, in the one kingdom of holiness and peace!

(Here may follow personal reflection or sharing of humble confession.)

8. Rite of Reconciliation

After the preceding preparation, the penitents are invited to kneel or to bow and say together a general formula for confession –for example, "I confess to almighty God . . . ." Then they may sing a suitable song to express heartfelt contrition and abiding trust in God's forgiving mercy. Or, they may listen to an exhortation like the following and join in the prayer which always concludes with the Lord's Prayer.

This is the Good News from God: the Father is healing, merciful Love. He takes the first step; reconciliation is his work from beginning to end. But only those who are willing to forgive and to heal experience the full power of his healing forgiveness.

If we are willing to forgive wholeheartedly, to set aside all resentment, and to accept our peace mission, then we are assured that our prayer will be heard. The prayer of the Church is a solemn, authoritative assurance that the sins of those who are merciful, who forgive and are peacemakers, stand surely forgiven — with the warning, however, that the sins of those who remain unforgiving stand unforgiven.

With this in mind, we pray together:

Father of all mercy, compassionate God,
you have sent us Jesus Christ to be our Reconciler,
our Divine Physician.
In his name we pray that the sins
of all those who have confessed,
of all those who want to be peacemakers,
may be thoroughly forgiven.
May their wounds be healed.
May they be thoroughly freed from enmity,
and open for the reign of love, of peace, and of justice.

O Lord,
through the apostle James,

you have assured us that the prayer of holy people
is powerful and effective.
So, as a community,
trusting that some of us are truly holy, we pray:
"Almighty God, have mercy on us,
forgive us our sins, and bring us to everlasting life."
Our Father . . . .

Another Prayer of Reconciliation

*This prayer is a free and shortened version of an ancient
Roman Preface used at the solemn celebration of reconciliation
on Holy Thursday. It was sung by the bishop while all, hand in
hand, walked in procession toward the altar. In and through
gratitude, we open our hearts to the gift of peace, and commit
ourselves to extend mercy to others in the same way that God
extends it to us.*

The Lord be with you!
  And with your spirit!
Let us lift up our hearts!
  We have lifted them up to the Lord!
Let us give thanks to the Lord!
  This is right and just!
All holy and merciful Father, it is our delightful duty
and our guiding light to wholeness, peace, and salvation,
to offer thanks to you always and on all occasions,
through your beloved Son, our Savior, Jesus Christ.

Gratefully we remember
the many signs and marvels of your mercy:
When our ancestors refused to honor you as God,
and did not offer thanks to you,
they drove themselves out from paradise.
But you did not abandon them.
In your great mercy you promised the coming Savior.

In all ages and everywhere,
you gave innumerable signs
of your healing forgiveness and mercy.
And in the fullness of time you sent us the great sign
of your compassionate mercy and your saving justice.
Jesus Christ, the Divine Physician, the Good Shepherd,
our Reconciler and our Peace;
and you associated with him the new Eve,
Mary, the Mother of Mercy.

With all who have experienced your mercy and saving justice
and have praised you
with a life of compassionate mercy and healing forgiveness,
with all the angels and saints, we praise your great name,
and commit ourselves to praise you by living lives
of compassionate love and saving justice
as peacemakers and reconcilers.
Our Father . . . .

*The priests now go to the places assigned for confession.
Penitents who desire to confess go to the priest of their choice.
After telling their sins and receiving suitable counsel, they are
given an appropriate penance and are absolved with the form
for the reconciliation of an individual penitent.*

*After the confessions have been heard, the priests return to
the sanctuary, and the presiding priest invites all to thank God
and praise him for his mercy. He then concludes the
celebration with a proclamation of praise to God, a prayer of
thanksgiving, a blessing, and words of farewell.*

Proclamation of Praise

(Mary's Canticle in Luke 1:46-55)

"My being proclaims the greatness of the Lord,
my spirit finds joy in God my savior,

For he has looked upon his servant in her lowliness;
   all ages to come shall call me blessed.
God who is mighty has done great things for me,
   holy is his name;
His mercy is from age to age on those who fear him.
"He has shown might with his arm;
   he has confused the proud in their inmost thoughts.
He has deposed the mighty from their thrones
   and raised the lowly to high places.
The hungry he has given every good thing,
   while the rich he has sent empty away.
He has upheld Israel his servant,
   ever mindful of his mercy;
Even as he promised our fathers,
   promised Abraham and his descendants forever."

Prayer of Thanksgiving

All-holy Father,
you have shown us your mercy
and made us a new creation
in the likeness of your Son.
Make us living signs of your love
for the whole world to see.
We ask this through Christ our Lord.
Amen.

9. The Blessing

May the blessing of almighty God,
the Father, and the Son, + and the Holy Spirit
come upon you and remain with you for ever.
Amen.

   *Here would be an appropriate place to give each other a sign
of peace, assurance of steadfast fidelity to the Lord's*

commandment to be compassionate and to forgive, and to fulfill the mission of peacemakers.

10. Words of Farewell

Let us go in peace and praise the Lord as peacemakers.
Response: We praise the Lord and give him thanks.